100
SASSY
TIPS
by **NICOLE**
SASSAMAN

PHOTOGRAPHY
Michael McCreary
Thomas Hencz
John Abeyta
Allison Hahn
Viktoria Saxby

Editor Roxanne Malcolm
Book design by Raimonda Tamosauskaite

First Edition 2013

ISBN 10: 1-419-66999-0
ISBN 13: 978-1-4196699-9-6

Library of Congress Control Number:
2007904096

Printed in China

To purchase additional copies of this book,
go to: www.nicolesassaman.com

100
SASSY TIPS
by Nicole Sassaman

For my sweet daughter, Ava.
You are my very best design yet!
I have so much fun doing everything
with you. Thank you for coming
into my life and making it sooooo
much better!

Love-
Mommy xxxooo

Who is Nicole Sassaman?

DESIGN AND GRACE

"For many years, I have enjoyed the sense of style, design and grace that Nicole has shared with me and those around her. I've even been lucky enough to be her "partner in crime" and see Nicole work her magic up-close and personal on a number of "design adventures" encompassing New York - San Francisco - Los Angeles and beyond. Whether it's tips on flower arranging, setting a table for a holiday event, re-framing a picture, wallpapering a room for a fresh look or a complete home remodel from top to bottom, I think you will find her unique and talented outlook fresh, new and exciting. I hope her book helps you to bring a touch of Nicole's Design Essence into your own life."

— **Doug Burton,** *Prospect Mortgage*

ARCHITECTURAL BEAUTY

"In my 30 year career selling houses, I learned it can be very tedious to satisfy buyers and sellers. Then walked in a beautiful woman that changed my life and extended my career. Nicole and I started out as strangers working together to meet our goal: "Sale - Sale". We did this together as a team and I can say, I learned a lot about perfection in all stages of construction, beginning with the tear down to the beautiful sight at the time of completion. Her ideas and sense of beauty are amazing, as you will see in this book. Nicole and her work are beautiful, but she is far more beautiful on the inside."

— **Marie Healey,** *John Aaroe Group*

BEYOND THE BOX

"As a home decorator, I am constantly assessing and exploring ideas. On a mission for furniture and products for a DIFFA (Design Industry Foundation Fighting Aids) Dining by Design project, Nicole walked into West Elm one morning, full of great ideas. Almost instantly, I knew I was in the presence of a multi-threat talent, a fabulous woman who offers her time and gifts so generously. Nicole does not think out of the box, rather she kicks the box over, opens it up, allowing you to tap into your own ideas, finding the designer within you."

— **Carlo Rios,** *retail home furnishings manager*

WHAT ROADBLOCKS?

"Nicole is the most innovative and forward thinking designer I have met yet. Her color choices and sense of aesthetics are impressive, but it's her solutions to the usual construction roadblocks that make you smack your head and think "Why didn't I think of that?"

— **Ken Nilsen,** *General Contractor, Malibu, CA*

FOR MY READERS

My philosophy is in truly knowing that anything is possible. From that angle, I come to the table with no limitations. So when I walk into a space, I assess what is there, but I also see what hasn't arrived yet, because in all of the things that we do, it is all about the possibilities. I never see what I don't have or can't do. My mind just isn't programmed like that. Instead, I look to see all of the opportunities that I can create from what I do have. Perhaps that is how I got the nickname of "Bugsy," who saw Las Vegas when everyone else only saw sand.

I love learning from what I do and all of the "happy accidents" along the way. Sharing this knowledge with you is the cherry on top for me! This book was made to share some very practical yet fun and creative tips which will be especially useful for those of you that are planning to do some renovations on your space. I hope that these ideas are helpful to you and even possibly spark a few new ones, as well.

I encourage you to look at design and everything else in your life from a slightly different perspective than you might normally be inclined. Open your eyes and know that mountains can be moved and that anything truly is possible and you will be surprised at the things that will come your way. If little old me can do this stuff, then so can you!

Designing Life!

Nicole

I am passing this wonderful writing of Desiderata on to you, as it is
very important to me and something that I use daily in all that I do.
Enjoy and share it with others.
It's good stuff!

xo– Nicole

Go placidly amidst the noise and haste, and remember what peace there may be in silence. As far as possible without surrender be on good terms with all persons. Speak your truth quietly and clearly; and listen to others, even the dull and the ignorant; they too have their story.

Avoid loud and aggressive persons, they are vexatious to the spirit. If you compare yourself with others, you may become vain and bitter; for always there will be greater and lesser persons than yourself.

Enjoy your achievements as well as your plans. Keep interested in your own career, however humble; it is a real possession in the changing fortunes of time.

Exercise caution in your business affairs; for the world is full of trickery. But let this not blind you to what virtue there is; many persons strive for high ideals; and everywhere life is full of heroism.

Be yourself. Especially, do not feign affection. Neither be cynical about love; for in the face of all aridity and disenchantment it is as perennial as the grass.

Take kindly the counsel of the years, gracefully surrendering the things of youth. Nurture strength of spirit to shield you in sudden misfortune. But do not distress yourself with dark imaginings. Many fears are born of fatigue and loneliness.

Beyond a wholesome discipline, be gentle with yourself. You are a child of the universe, no less than the trees and the stars; you have a right to be here.

And whether or not it is clear to you, no doubt the universe is unfolding as it should. Therefore be at peace with God, whatever you conceive Him to be, and whatever your labors and aspirations, in the noisy confusion of life keep peace with your soul. With all its sham, drudgery, and broken dreams, it is still a beautiful world. Be cheerful.

Strive to be happy.
- Max Ehrmann

TABLE
CON
TENTS
of

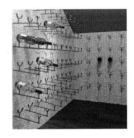

kitchens

The kitchen somehow always finds a way to be the hub of the house. People love to gather and socialize around great food and drink, so it makes sense that everyone ends up in the kitchen. What a wonderful place it is. Whether you are creating delightful and edible creations, eating them or sharing them with a friend, you are creating an amazing life moment. No matter if your space is big or small, it is incredibly important to put a great amount of thought into the design and layout of your kitchen. It should be **functional, inspirational** and **comfortable** to socialize in a way that speaks to you. Make a list of everything that you want it to be, and I'll bet you can find a way to turn it into a reality!

No. 01
FORM MEETS FUNCTION

The kitchen is often a gathering place for conversation. I created a larger work space and extra seating for such occasions. This way people can be in the kitchen, but sitting and comfortable.

BEFORE ↧

No. 02
ARCHITECTURAL CLEANUP

Removing excess archways and columns is an example of how simple it can be to clean up and open a space. It changed the look from 1980's Italian to a more architectural and clean-lined look of today.

BEFORE ⊺

No. 03
STRETCHING STYLE

If you fall in love with an expensive tile or stone that is out of your budget, just use it for a backsplash instead of an entire wall. Your money will go further and you will still get the look that won your heart.

BEFORE ⊥

No. 04
BRINGING IT TOGETHER

Sometimes sacrificing extra storage for an open, entertaining kitchen can be a fruitful trade-off. The cabinetry wood was used on the ceiling above the bar and helped define the space. It broke up the white ceiling and created a more finished look.

BEFORE ⬍

No. 05
SIMPLE LIGHTING

Using clear pendant lights like these is a great way to add extra lighting while still keeping the space light and open. Simplicity is often the perfect choice to define just the right style.

No. 06
DETAILED DOORS

For a unique and slightly industrial touch, the inserts of the upper cabinets are window screens over white frosted glass to keep the dust out. ↥

No. 07
CHALKBOARD FUN!

I covered the 9' pocket door separating the kitchen from the entryway in chalkboard paint. Also, try it on a wall or closet doors in a child's room. This can create a really fun element in any space! ↦

Look for the formula for chalkboard paint on page 225

No. 08
CLEAN & NARROW

The recessed handles in the cabinets are a streamlined look and one less thing to bump into in a narrow kitchen like this. Also, using shelves instead of cabinets above the sink creates a more open feel and is both stylish and functional.

BEFORE

No. 9
ELIMINATING SOFFITS

Dropping the ceiling height to meet the soffit helped to define the kitchen area and to get rid of the soffits altogether. This new flush ceiling was a very simple solution to clean up the lines in the space.

BEFORE ↧

No. 10
LIGHTING DIVIDER

Installing pendant lights in a row like this is a great way to add style, lighting and to create a subtle sense of division between spaces. They really help to define an area.

BEFORE ⊢→

No. 11
FULL HEIGHT FINISH

When designing your kitchen, be sure to find ways to expand the room rather than chop it up. Here, I took the backsplash tile all the way above the cabinets to the ceiling and even around all of the windows. This creates a much more finished look and expands the space by not breaking it up with additional materials.

BEFORE I

No. 12
ADDED SEATING

Need more seating in the kitchen?
Try adding a raised bar to a counter or island. The hardware used to
attach the bar to the counter allows
an open and airy look and main-
tains the counter space below. ⇡

No. 13
ORGANIZED STYLE

Don't forget about finishing off
the insides of your cabinets.
This is an added expense, but
it looks so much nicer and it
generally doubles the amount
of storage space, as well. ↪

No. 14
CREATIVE CABINETS

If you are looking for an industrial look, try using tool cabinets made for the garage in your kitchen! Think outside of the box and use ordinary things in extraordinary ways. I have seen beautiful Asian armoires turned into food pantries. Open your mind to all of the possibilities! ↑

No. 15
DECORATIVE NICHES

In this kitchen I designed for the set of "Extra", I created fun nooks on the front side of the island. I tiled the back panel to match the back splash and also added accent lights. A lovely way to showcase prized kitchenware. Details like this are easy to do and can really make your space come to life! ↦

bathrooms

Bathrooms have taken on a new and much sassier role in a home. As people have become far more design savvy, they expect their bathrooms to become more of a spa. There are so many fabulous bathroom finishes and fixtures today that can truly personalize the space and make it extraordinary. When designing your powder room, remember that, like the dining room, it is the other space in the home where you can take an extra chance or two. Do you hang a chandelier in it, or perhaps you spend a little more on a cool sink or vanity to make a statement? Treat yourself to thinking the design of your bathroom through and make it more than a place where you simply take a shower. Turn it into your retreat and a place where you pamper yourself from head to toe!

No. 16
REPLACING FIXTURES

Changing this sink into a floating vanity with an interesting vessel sink like this teak one, along with updating the toilet, made for a 360 degree transformation here. This is an easy and cost-saving choice. These touches really help to finish off your space perfectly and make it uniquely yours.

BEFORE ↧

No. 17
DESIGNER DETAIL

When preparing the walls for the new tile, a long nook on the bathtub wall is easy to frame. This is such a fabulous detail that can serve as a place to set soaps or your favorite candles. Continuing the tiled wall behind the sink and toilet can hide unforeseen glitches that often appear during remodeling.

BEFORE ⌐

No. 18
STYLISH STORAGE

Here, I was able to find some space in the wall to create a very large medicine cabinet. I switched the three windows above it to one long one in order to be in line with the medicine cabinet and then covered the remaining walls in a decorative mosaic tile to create both style and storage!

BEFORE ⅂

No. 19
STEALING SPACE

This bathroom doubled in size by incorporating its small adjacent hallway. I'll often absorb a compact closet or portion of a hallway to increase the area of the proximate room. Hallways can be a great waste of space, so always look to see if you can incorporate them within a room.

No. 20
GLASS TILE SAVIOR!

Before grouting glass tiles, rinse them with hot and then cold water a few times. Since they can have a tendency to crack from the temperature changes, it will likely happen then and be easier to replace before grouting.

BEFORE ⊢→

No. 21
CUSTOMIZING SINKS

A sink like this can be made out of slabs. Your fabricator can create it out of the same slab as your counters or a different one, if you want contrast. They can custom the size, shape, and style for you to create your own unique piece.

No. 22
SALVAGING SPACE

Sometimes there doesn't seem to be enough room to house both a separate shower and bathtub in one room. Think outside of the box and see if the tub can go in the middle of the room. Or what about right in front of the shower, like this one? Remember that a tub doesn't really need a wall. Today, your plumbing can be mounted on the floor, so there are many options in creating a unique and flexible bathroom.

No. 23
COMPLETE SPLASH

Don't limit fabulous tile to just the backsplash. Carry the stone from the ceiling to the floor. This wall of stone gives a rustic feel to this sleek bath. Behind the mirror and under the vanity is accent lighting to set the perfect mood when all other lights are off, while highlighting the stone.

BEFORE ↧

No. 24
PERFECTLY HIDDEN DRAIN

The teak wood on the floor and ceiling of the shower adds contrast and warmth next to sleek finishes. This can be added to almost any shower floor as a separate piece that can be set in over the slab and to also hide the drain. Wrapping the stone around the shower wall into the dressing area also increases the sense of flow.

BEFORE ⬇

No. 25
DESIGNER DOORS

Using glass inserts in your interior doors is a smart way to add light from one space to the next. Take the time to design the details of your interior doors. Choosing to create these 3-light doors is so much more interesting than the standard 1-light doors. 1

No. 26
BRING THE OUTSIDE IN

Installing a stone that is typically used outdoors in your interior is a great way to add a rustic feel to your modern space. It also adds so much more interest and depth to a space. ↦

No. 27
FRAMELESS FUSION

Changing out old framed shower doors to frameless ones is a quick and easy way to update a shower. And don't be afraid to use mosaic tiles like this on a bathroom floor. It is a wonderful look and it provides a lot of traction so that slipping is less likely.

BEFORE ⌐

No. 28
DECORATIVE LIGHTING

Hanging a chandelier in the middle of your bathroom can be a great way to add light, style and to help anchor in your space. There are so many amazing decorative fixtures available today. They can add such drama to your space!

BEFORE ⟂

No. 29
FABULOUS FIXTURES

Look for interesting plumbing fixtures. In today's
market there are some amazing choices that can
truly make a lasting impression. This one is simple,
sleek and sexy! How and where you install them
can make all of the difference, so think it through.

No. 30
FUNCTIONAL ART

Choosing interesting objects like the bronze hands-turned-towel-hooks can make your space more personal. These little hands came from a trip that the homeowners took to Bali and each time that they see them, they are reminded of their amazing journey.

No. 31
LUMINOUS LIGHTING

Adding warm light pendants will soften shadows on the face from overhead lighting. It is also a nice way to add dimension and more detail to your design.

BEFORE ↦

No. 32
WARM STORAGE

A warming drawer for your towels is the ultimate in luxury. Kitchen warmers have exposed heating elements. For fire safety, be sure to use a drawer made for the bath. ↑

No. 33
SPACE SAVING SEATING

A flip-down teak shower bench is amazing for small shower spaces. It attaches to the wall and folds up to save space when not in use. It also creates a very spa-like feel. ↦

No. 34
IMPECCABLE SINKS

Vanities in a bathroom are critically important to the space. When you go to create the vanity, think beyond the box! Do you need to buy a separate sink? Actually, your fabricator can integrate your sink into your counters and all of the materials can be made from the very same slab of stone. If you choose to do this, you can take it one step further and hide the drain under the slab like this. Be sure to choose plumbing fixtures that support the flow of this design choice. Decisions like these is what creates a sexy and streamlined look that leaves a lasting impression.

No. 35
SMART REMODEL

The ledge tiled in glass mosaic brings the perfect amount of style and function to this shower. It can be a simple way to update materials in an old shower without a full remodel! If you have the space in your shower, you can frame a wall ledge like this into it and cover with a fun decorative tile. This creates a great function and adds so much style!

No. 36
SAVING LOST SPACE

Knowledge is power. Knowing
if there is space inside of a
wall that you can capture can
really help you to enhance
your design. Here, behind
this bathtub, extra space was
used to frame out this beautiful niche for shampoos and
soaps. Nice added detail!

No. 37
WATCH YOUR BACK!

When selecting a vessel sink that will be used in front of a mirrored backsplash, be sure the back of the sink is also glazed, as most are unfinished. Please learn from my mistakes! ↥ ↦

No. 38
INTERESTING EDGE

A rough-cut edge on the stone countertop ties in with the shower tile and adds a pastoral element to this sleek bath. Try a rough edge like this to create a unique detail to any space. ↦

No. 39
FUNCTIONAL PRIVACY

When you need to build a wall or even a half wall like this one, be sure to think it a step further and ask yourself if the wall should be storage or have some interesting display nook in it. In most cases, when you see a small dividing wall like this, it is framed and covered with drywall. That is valuable space that could be used as storage! In this case, I took a little bit of space from each side and created storage and display areas. Taking it a step further and wrapping the piece with wood gave it a much more polished look. You could also use stone, glass, tile and so many other finishes in an instance like this. You could even add some lighting!

bedrooms

Your bedroom is a place to rest and rejuvenate your soul on so many levels. It is a room that no matter what colors and styles you use to create it, there should always be some sense of calm in it. We spend more time in our bedrooms than any other room in the house. The world is coming at us from so many different directions, that when the time arrives for you to lay your head on the pillow at night, you should feel like you are in the most comfortable sanctuary of peace that is all yours. Find patterns and colors that blend with your very being. Pay close attention to your lighting and be sure to have several mood settings, even if it is just a dimming lamp next to your bed! Design a bedroom that speaks to every aspect of your soul!

No. 40
COMBINING FORCES

I was able to turn these two rooms into one master suite by knocking down the wall between them and moving the fireplace to the opposite wall. It allowed so much more light into the room, while enlarging the overall space and enhancing the view.

BEFORE ⥥

No. 41
CREATING UNITY

Bi-folding doors allow the inside and out to mingle, while complimenting flooring and sturdy exterior curtains add to this cabana-like patio adjacent to the master bedroom. Now you feel like you are on a vacation while sipping your morning coffee!

↤ BEFORE

No. 42
FLOORING FLOW

Choosing your indoor and outdoor flooring to be similar in color and pattern for adjacent spaces like this can make the them feel as one large space. This makes a big difference whether the doors are open or closed.

← BEFORE

No. 43
ENHANCED EXTERIOR

Building a deck around the back of this master suite gave it a whole added dimension of looks and usability. I replaced the windows with bi-folding doors to create a sense of oneness with the outdoors. If you can't add to interior area, always look to see if you can add or enhance the outside space.

BEFORE ↦

No. 44
OVERCOMING OBSTACLES

Two small bedrooms became this multifunctional master suite. Now it's an office, den and place to sleep. Try to find a way to make an obstacle part of your design. The load-bearing column between the desks created a nice separation between the two work spaces. These obstacles can often become the best part of a room, so keep an open mind.

BEFORE ⏐

No. 45
PRISTINE PURPOSE

This fireplace was desperate for a makeover. Given that it consumed a large corner of the room, it needed to function more as a showpiece. I reframed the area for the new fire box with a recessed nook for the flat screen television. Now it has more functionality and style!

BEFORE ⌶

No. 46
THE DEVIL IN THE DETAILS

When using this type of stacked stone, there is no need for grout if it's installed with precision. It will actually have a much more natural look without it. Be sure to have your installer miter all edges where there is a corner or edge for a more professional and finished look.

BEFORE ⌐

No. 47
SLEEK STORAGE

Creating a built-in bed, as I did here, really allows for a more streamlined look and is simple enough to do. It is much cleaner-looking than a bed with separate bedside tables on each end. You can also take the opportunity to make the base of the bed a wonderful way to store things by creating drawers underneath the mattress on either side of the bed.

← BEFORE

No. 48
INTERESTING INSTALL

Using ordinary things in extraordinary ways is often the best
design tip there is. The stone that
was used around this fireplace
was beautiful on it's own, but the
installation of it made all of the
difference. Instead of installing it
flat on the wall for a flush finish, I
was able to create some dimension by building some of the tiles
out further than others. This type
of install takes some thought and
time, but the result makes for
a far more interesting look. You
can apply this technique with
stone tiles almost anywhere!

No. 49
MAKING IT TWO FOR ONE

Applying the same concept in creating a built-in headboard also works great in a situation like this where one headboard and table can service two twin-sized beds. As you can see, this made the room look so much larger and function much better.

BEFORE ⊺

No. 50
A ROOM WITH A VIEW

Sometimes small changes can make the biggest difference. Creating large glass window openings from floor to ceiling can add so much light and beauty and truly make your space look much larger. Even if you look out to a building next door, you can plant some beautiful bamboo outside of the window and achieve the same open feeling.

BEFORE ⊺

No. 51
DRESS TO IMPRESS

Extend your bedroom by installing cabinets in your closet to compliment the furniture in your bedroom. It really pays to spend a little extra on backing the cabinets rather than seeing the drywall, as well. Some of us spend a great deal of time in our closet contemplating what to wear. Why not make it a rich and inviting place?

BEFORE ⌐

No. 52
FULL HEIGHT CLOSET

Removing the soffits in this closet allowed me to run the cabinets much higher and create more storage. Every little bit counts, so be sure to maximize the space that you do have in your closet. Increasing the height of the cabinets also created a much grander look and feel.

BEFORE

living rooms

Living Rooms have become much like the kitchen with more and more open floor plans being used. The space has turned into a room where people tend to gather together to socialize and relax. It is a room that has become **the jack knife of all rooms** in a home, as it can be a meeting place, a media room, a game room, a place to eat dinner, play, read, etc. With all of these potential uses, it has made us think through the design of the room a bit more carefully than we used to. Remember to **think outside of the box.** Be sure to mix equal parts of **smart, sass and style** in this room and really think through the many wonderful ways that you will utilize the space to make it everything your heart desires!

No. 53
WIDE OPEN WALLS

The old fireplace was removed to add the wall of glass bi-fold doors that overlook the pool and grounds. I created this new custom fireplace and it is the crowning jewel of the family room now. It remains a dancing focal point even when changing out all of the furnishings. Think of how you can design unique fireplaces to create a more architectural feel.

BEFORE ↓

No. 54
PUSH OF A BUTTON

When a room calls for multiple window shades, save time when opening and closing them by installing remote-controlled motorized units. You will find that they will be open more often if all it requires is the push of a button.

BEFORE ↨

No. 55
FABULOUS FINISH

The finish on the new entertainment center is nothing more than the brown coating used beneath stucco, but smoothed out to look like concrete. The recessed lights in the wooden shelves are a great touch to create dramatic detail in the evenings. You can create a wonderful look without spending a lot of money on materials by using stucco like this instead of stone or tile.

BEFORE ⌐

No. 56
INTERIOR EXPANSION

Eliminating the balcony in this high rise condominium not only adds more livable square footage, the floor-to-ceiling glass allows the view to become part of the room. Think through your design to see if you can capture some outdoor space and incorporate it as part of the interior area to create a more livable and usable room.

BEFORE ⌶

No. 57
DEFINING SPACE

Using rugs like this can really help in defining your space when you have large open areas. It also creates a much cozier area. Carpet stores can customize most sizes for you, which gives you unlimited options and styles to choose from.

No. 58
FUNCTIONING FIREPLACE

Finishing off this fireplace by framing some wood above the mantle to recess the television and create a nook for a sculpture with light made all of the difference in looks and function. Making the two surfaces flush also created a cleaner look. This can save you in a renovation from having to remove what might already be a beautiful mantel piece. Look to see if you can simply add to what is already there to build a new look and save yourself a lot of time and money.

BEFORE ⌐

No. 59
QUIET ELEGANCE

When something is as stunning as this, sometimes it is best to keep it simple. You don't always need a mantel over a fireplace. This tile is so beautiful that along with the simplicity of the design, it makes the fireplace into a piece of art of its own. There is no need to break up such beauty with a mantel or piece of art hanging over it. The look and feel of this is quiet elegance all the way and deserves to remain just that.

No. 60
COVERING IT UP

I added chunky molding around the old metal frame of the window. It completely revived it and was far less expensive than replacing the entire window. If you can't replace old windows, think about finding clever ways to hide the old frames like this. You can update them without costing you the time and money of replacing them all together.

← BEFORE

No. 61
EXTENDED MANTEL

If you have a fireplace on a larger wall, take a look to see if you should extend the materials around your fireplace box in order to create a more dramatic design and truly showcase your fireplace. Here, I was able to take all of the space to the right of the box and that created an area that screamed for this open cabinet to hang. This allowed a place to display pictures and things that you might normally put on the upper mantel and created such a fantastic look!

No. 62
MATERIAL DIFFERENCE

Choosing eye-catching stone is the perfect finishing touch to a fireplace area like this. It makes it the focal piece that it should be rather than leaving it in a plain drywall finish. Take the time to choose something special for areas like this.

No. 63
REFINISHING FIXTURES

Paint can surely achieve wonders! New stain on the wood floors and a fresh white coat on the cabinets transformed this outdated den. My favorite tip here is in using paint for high heat areas like barbecues to spray lighting fixtures like these rather than replacing them altogether. The brass light fixtures here were simply sprayed with paint right in place, and voila!

BEFORE ꜱ

No. 64
NICHE DISPLAY WALL

Creating niches in a wall like this can be a great way to add style and lighting to what may end up to be a boring old wall. I always urge you to investigate what space might be hiding in a wall that may be a wonderful opportunity to add a design element like this.

No. 65
ARCHITECTURAL LIGHTING

Use space between studs to create architectural interest.
Grabbing unused space in a ceiling may require you to frame
around studs, plumbing, and who knows what else, but it can be
so worth it because of the height you can add to the room. It is
a wonderful opportunity to house some lighting in, as well.

No. 66
FLOATING FIREPLACE

There are so many different ways to design fireplaces today, between the unique materials there are to use and the fireboxes that are available. How you install them can make all of the difference. Why not try floating the entire thing above the floor? It is a great way to create a more modern and open feel and it is very simple to do. In fact, this particular installation is a great solution when adding a fireplace as an afterthought. There are quite a few fireplaces that vent out the back now rather than having to go through the roof. This opens up your design to putting a fireplace like this in almost any place of your home.

dining rooms

Ahhh... what a wonderful room to create memories in! Whether you eat in your dining room every day or just for certain occasions, it is a very special space to be in. The dining room is a place that gets everyone to sit down at the same time and share fabulous food and memories. When it comes to design, it is oftentimes the room where you can take a few chances and do something unique and special. Should the walls be red or covered in a crazy pattern of wallpaper? Is the light fixture a little piece of art on its own? Should it have silver leaf ceiling? Be sure to create a space that supports the energy that you would like to create during these times. Style has many flavors. Make it your very own!

No. 67
COURAGE & COLOR

Don't be afraid to use dark colors in a room. The green grass wallpaper adds texture to this space and makes a cozier feel. The dark blue-green paint on the ceiling anchors the space and creates a nice splash of color. People always think that dark colors make a room look small. When used properly, they can simply make it warmer and add a tremendous amount of style! Be fearless about using color in your designs!

BEFORE ⌐

No. 68
THE OLD AND THE NEW

Don't hesitate to mix modern
furnishings with antiques. In this
space most of the furniture was
modern. I added the Chinese
console and Asian accessories
for an eclectic feel. Go for it
and include pieces in your
space that really speak to you,
regardless of convention.

No. 69
FINISHING TOUCH

The makeover here was all about changing the finishes and adding two details. I simply stained the existing wood a darker gray/ brown tone and covered the walls in a silver grasscloth. Then, I added an inexpensive lighting fixture which I was able to make look a bit richer by mirroring the wooden valance at the window that I added around the base of it. This tied in both elements beautifully and cost very little to do, while continuing to use the newly stained wood to create a nice sense of flow in the design.

BEFORE ⬍

offices

Most of us spend a fare amount of time in our offices, so it is important that they really support who we are and what we want to do. Be sure to get clear on that one! Create an environment that **embodies your passions** and your successes will most likely multiply themselves as a result. It's almost magical! Never have your back to the door and no matter what it takes - **keep it organized!** Make sure that each element is well thought out and that even the art **reflects something inspirational** and meaningful to you. You are important and so is the work that you do here. Design a space that supports that and everything will work out just fine!

No. 70
CURVACEOUS CURE

The gray finish on the fireplace is the brown coating typically used under stucco. This was a perfect choice for saving the rounded curves on this fireplace, as tile or stone could have been much more limiting. Try adding stucco dye for more color possibilities or even paint over it.

No. 71
DETAILING BLINDS

I chose a coordinating fabric band on the wooden blinds of this office as another way to tie the room's color palette together. These little details can truly make all of the difference!

BEFORE ↦

No. 72
REFLECTING BACK

Mirror the back of shelving to give more dimension and volume to a room. It is easy and very cost-effective to do. You can also use many other shades of mirror. Maybe something a bit smoky or copper-toned would be a nice fit for your design?

BEFORE ⌶

No. 73
STONE-WALLED EFFECT

Using stacked stone like this was the perfect choice in creating a rustic and more finished look in the reception area and the conference room of this office. Before turning to paint, look to see if covering small walls like these in an interesting stone or tile might be a more stylish and fitting solution.

No. 74
FINE FURNISHINGS

Incorporating your office into
another room like this living
room can be a perfect solution
as long as you make sure that
your furnishings between the
two spaces flow. This office is a
stylish addition to the living room
and works beautifully as a result.

sound studio

Not everyone in the world has their very own sound studio, but a few lucky ones do. Quite a few people do have spaces that they specifically use as a specialty area to fulfill a passion. Whether it is a sewing room, an art studio, a writer's retreat or a play room, making these special areas in a home matter is very important. These are rooms created just to house one's enthusiasm over something that rings true to them in every ounce of their mind, body and soul. So guess what? The area must inspire the user to bring their visions into realities. Make every step of your design in these spaces matter. Every element of the space should support the goal that the artist is trying to achieve, especially if it is a playroom for your five year old!

No. 75
BEAUTIFUL FUNCTION

The walls and ceilings throughout this studio are fully functioning acoustic panels. The wall panels are covered with rich tactile fabrics. The wood floors and trim are stained a slight tint of gray. These evoke a masculine yet inviting atmosphere. When designing around things that need to function, be sure that you don't compromise the design. It is important that these elements incorporate your color palette and enhance your designs.

↵ BEFORE

No. 76
SMART SQUARES

Stylish carpet squares in a heavy traffic area of this sound studio help keep this space looking fresh. If one gets worn, it's effortless to replace the square.

No. 77
DRAMATIC DISPLAY

Finding clever ways to display collections of things like these guitars in this recording studio was the perfect answer to make an artistic statement, show off the collection and store the guitars all at the same time. Grab some unused space in a wall and look what you can do.

the details

It is ever so true that the Devil is indeed in the details! In the building and design world, the quality of every move that is made and every design element that is created hinges on these details. Do not rush the creative process. Each aspect of every little thing in any one space matters. We may not notice each one, but as a whole, your project cannot come together with a completed, stylish and finished look unless you detail the space properly. This can be making sure the finishes are installed properly, to creating custom doors and hardware, to floating your cabinets for a more open and unique look. The details that you can create in a space are truly endless and however far you take them be sure to create a flavor all your own!

No. 78
GORGEOUS FINISHES

Tile isn't just for the bathroom and kitchen. In this entry, the doorway wall and inside the display nooks are tiled. It adds so much style and protects the walls in an area with high traffic at the same time.

BEFORE ⬇

No. 79
EVERY INCH COUNTS

Eliminate unused space. Replacing this stepping drywall detail with a rich built-in display area took advantage of the height and added interest to the stairwell. Look at your space to see if there are opportunities like this screaming to be utilized.

BEFORE ↓

No. 80
STUNNING STAIRWAYS

Stairways can be such a wonderful opportunity to add style to any space. Creating a unique pattern with metal can create a very special look. Even drywall can be quite extraordinary when done in a unique way like this. Turn your stairway into a piece of art!

No. 81
SNEAK IN STORAGE

Always make the most of a small niche in your space. This cabinet provides a lot of storage and style, and wallpapering the small wall above it is the perfect touch to finish it off!

No. 82
MULTIPURPOSE STORAGE

Storage at a premium? These bench seats are now hinged for extra storage. Just another reminder to look for unused space in your walls for storage and design opportunities like this.

BEFORE ⇲

No. 83
CELLAR STORAGE

Even if you don't have the space for a wine cellar, it doesn't mean that you can't create the look and feel of one! Here, by creating a cabinet from floor to ceiling and simply installing the hardware for the bottles to rest inside of, I was able to instantly create the look and feel of a wine cellar. This cabinet was tucked perfectly behind the bar, but you could apply the same concept in a kitchen or on a wall by itself. It is a simple way to create a fantastic look!

No. 84
STAIRCASE STORAGE

Get creative with unused space. I turned a boring coat closet into a beautiful wine cellar under this staircase. This cellar is directly opposite the formal dining room and makes for a great conversation piece. It makes you feel like you are eating in a wine cellar!

↩ BEFORE

No. 85
DOUBLE DUTY SHELVES

These custom wine holders made of solid walnut are a great idea for upper shelves in a kitchen, as they can also hold stacks of plates or decorative items.

No. 86
DRAMATIC DOORS

Doors are expensive no matter what, so think about taking the design a step further in your space and create something custom and special like these doors. The hardware that you choose can make or break them, so choose wisely.

No. 87
SIMPLE WINE CELLAR

An easy and effective way to
create a wine cellar like this
is to simply buy metal wine
bottle racks and install them
into the walls. Finishing the
walls first with a stone like this
will make the cellar look more
professional and elegant.

No. 88
ARTISTIC HALLWAY

Constructing nooks like these is easy to do.
They are notched in between the wall's two-
by-four studs. Adding a recessed light at the
top is a nice detail along with a wood, stone,
or glass ledge. You can even add mirror to
the back to open up the space a bit. ↑

No. 89
CREATING LIGHT BOXES

If you would like to create an architectural look like
these interesting little window boxes, you can frame
these out in most interior and exterior walls to end
up with this effect. These windows can be placed
between most studs, so even if the wall is structural,
you can generally frame them out with no issues. This
creates an amazing look while letting tons of light
in. You can use clear or decorative glass, too. ↦

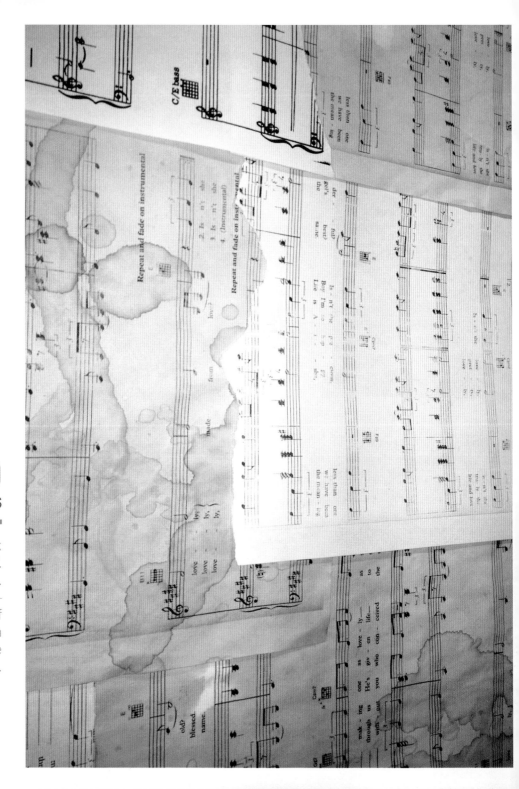

No. 90
CREATIVE WALL COVERINGS

Wallpaper doesn't have to break the bank if you create it yourself. Here, old sheet music was used. You could use old menus, wrapping paper, newspaper, etc. If you are renting, you could even achieve the same look in a more temporary fashion with tape.

No. 91
BACKLIGHTING MIRRORS

When creating the vanity in your bathroom, don't forget about the mirror and the lighting. This is a perfect example of how you can combine two in one. Rather than hanging a mirror on the wall, I designed this one to be recessed and floated the mirror off the wall so that I could backlight it for a sexier look. How you finish off the wall behind the mirror and around it can only enhance your design. You could use drywall, wood, mosaic tiles, stones, frosted glass, etc. Make the time to take your design one step further and it will make all of the difference!

No. 92
NARROW FLOATING LEDGE

This decorative ledge is a great way to add style, dimension and even create a narrow shelf for accessories in any hallway. You could cover the front of it with glass and replace the rocks with a collection that you might have, like wine corks, match boxes, etc.

No. 93
FULL BAR EXTENSION

Extending this closet-like bar and turning it into a serving bar with bar stools was a simple solution to maximizing this area and making it a better place to entertain. Waterfalling the countertop down the side of the bar is another way to create a modern design and adding recessed lights under the shelves behind the bar is the perfect finishing touch.

BEFORE ↧

outdoors

The outdoor space of a home is as essential as the inside. The key to success in dealing with your outdoor space, even if it is a patio at a condominium, is to make the transition between the inside of the home and the outside as seamless as possible. No matter what the weather is like, you should feel as though you are one with both spaces. This area is an opportunity for you to create another space to live in or an area that inspires you in some way. The outside should reflect some sort of energy to the inside of your home and enhance everything. It can set a mood like nothing else, so be sure to look for opportunities to bring the outside in and the inside out whenever you can! This shift in design creates such an impact on you, so make it matter!

No. 94
COLOR CONCRETE

All of the concrete was tinted with a stain in an ebony color. It is applied with a roller just like house paint. You can also put dye in your concrete mix before you pour it to add color. This is a great option for any concrete floor, including the garage, to add a bit of style without much expense. ↑

No. 95
CREATE A CABANA

Extend your living space. By enclosing a patio with outdoor curtains and hardware it is easy to turn any covered patio into its very own cabana. ↦

No. 96
OUT OF THIN AIR

The new retaining walls for the pool and grass terrace below required truck loads of back-fill dirt and hundreds of man hours. Since this was a slightly remote location, I provided the crew with daily lunches. They appreciated the gesture and kept the project on time.
In return, I turned air into a pool and a yard. All things are possible!

↤ BEFORE

UNIQUE POOL TILE

Carry your style outdoors. Accessorize your pool with glamorous tile before turning to traditional pool tiles. Most of the same tiles that you would enjoy in your beautiful kitchen or bathrooms are durable enough for your pool.

No. 98
SMART & STYLISH SAFETY

Keeping child safety in mind, this pool was reshaped to meet the limitations of a new motorized pool cover that tucks away neatly under the pool's edge. This was a great way to achieve both form and function, so think through your pool design for things like this before you begin to build.

BEFORE ⌐

No. 99
FLEXIBLE FURNISHINGS

Remove old built-ins that don't function properly and replace them with furnishings that offer you more options depending on how you are entertaining.

BEFORE ⏌

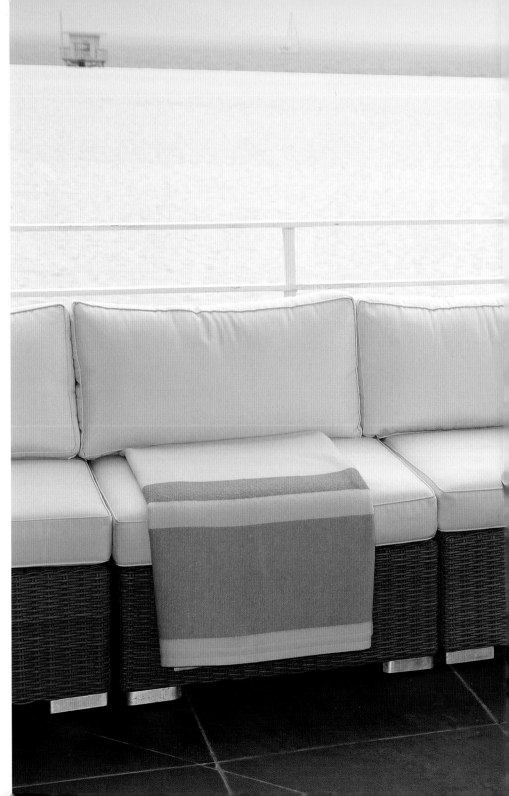

No. 100
FREESTANDING FIRE

This is a wonderful example of how you can create something out of nothing. This would have normally just been a patio overlooking a fence into the house next door. With a little design savvy, it became so much more by creating a separation between the home with this freestanding fireplace. It also created a place to hide the grill behind! All you need is a gas line and the space to do this and you can create the same look that anchors in the space and creates a warm gathering area to entertain and relax.

Chalkboard Paint Recipe

Start with flat-finish latex paint in any shade. For small areas, such as a door panel, mix 1 cup at a time.

1. Pour 1 cup of paint into a container. Add 2 tablespoons of <u>unsanded</u> tile grout. Mix with a paint stirrer, carefully breaking up clumps.

2. Apply paint with a roller or a sponge paintbrush to a primed or painted surface. Work in small sections, going over the same spot several times to ensure full, even coverage. Let dry.

3. Smooth area with 150-grit sandpaper and wipe off dust.

4. To condition: Rub the side of a piece of chalk over entire surface. Wipe away residue with a barely damp sponge.

ENJOY!

ACKNOWLEDGMENTS

Thank you to my "Dream Team." I couldn't do it without you and I so appreciate your artistry. Every one of you is so special to me. You are like family to me and aside from your talent, I enjoy the journey that we take together on each project. I care so much about each of you and appreciate you beyond what words can express. Thank you for all of your hard work, can-do attitude, talent, and creativity! On Team Sassy you make it possible for there to be "no problems, just solutions"!

Thank you Marie Healey, my real estate specialist, my long time dear friend and woman who has been like a mother to me. Together we always turn lemons into lemonade and then we have so much fun drinking it!

I especially want to thank my late mother, Judith Ann, my father, John, and my late Grandmother Dorothy for keeping the flame of my creative spirit on fire. Each of you in so many ways encouraged me to never take no for an answer and to always find a way to make the things that I wanted come to life. You taught me that every wall truly is a door. I thank you from the deepest part of my being, as without your wonderful lessons, I would never have the courage to fail and try the crazy things that I do! xoxo!

Most of the designs in this book are things that I created, but there are a few that I thought were so Sassy, I borrowed them from some of my friends who were gracious enough to share. Thanks to my very Sassy and stylish friends for your fun designs: Ian Aaron, Tom Sudinsky, Ron Maassen, Mark Leventen, Emily & Philip Klaparta, Russell Mitchell and Tom Dunlap and Doug Burton at Casa Burlap.

Thank you to Raimonda for creating this amazing book and showcasing these spaces in such a well thought out and beautiful way. You are unbelievably talented and I love working with you!

RESOURCES

Walker Zanger
Viking Range Corporation
Williams Sonoma
Rolling Greens
Jonathan Adler
Blueprint
Poliform
Restoration Hardware
Waterworks
Ann Sacks
Holly Hunt
Details
Mitchell Gold
HD Buttercup
Bulthaup
Silestone
Miele
SieMatic
Poltrona Frau
Malibu Market and Design
Ferguson
NanaWall
Montigo Fireplaces
Crate and Barrel
West Elm
J & M Blinds
Maxalto
Diva
B&B Italia
The Carpet Studio
Anawalt Lumber
Koontz Hardware
Board Brokers